THE LITTLE BOOK OF
KOBE

First published in 2021 by OH!
An Imprint of Welbeck Non-Fiction Limited,
part of Welbeck Publishing Group.
Offices in: London – 20 Mortimer Street, London W1T 3JW
and Sydney – Level 17, 207 Kent St, Sydney NSW 2000 Australia
www.welbeckpublishing.com

ISBN 978-1-91161-096-0

Compiled by: Chas Newkey-Burden
Editorial: Theresa Bebbington
Project manager: Russell Porter
Design: James Pople
Production: Jess Brisley

A CIP catalogue record for this book is available from the Library of Congress

Printed in China

10 9 8 7 6

THE LITTLE BOOK OF
KOBE

IN HIS OWN WORDS

CONTENTS

INTRODUCTION

Kobe Bryant was one of sport's most accomplished and outspoken figures. His extraordinary life story is one of obsession, determination, and burning self-confidence, as he rose to the top like a meteor, willing to destroy anything that got in his way.

Playing his entire 20-year career with the Los Angeles Lakers, he won two league scoring titles as well as the five championship rings. His achievements also include being the 2008 NBA Most Valuable Player (MVP) and two-time NBA Finals' MVP. During his dazzling decades in the game, he was twice an Olympic champion.

After retiring in 2016, he applied his driven, meticulous energy to the worlds of business and charity. In the final years of his life, he became a formidable brand builder, generous investor, and a direct inspiration to athletes and CEOs alike. He supported a host of good causes, helping the homeless and those battling cancer.

Never a man to hold his tongue, Kobe's thoughts could be as entertaining as watching him on the court. His words were inspiring, hilarious, and confrontational. In fact, his philosophies became such an integral part of his brand that he named them the "Mamba Mentality."

The quotes in the pages that follow represent the essence of a strong-willed and focused man who was unafraid to tell the universe what he thought of it. You will also find some of the heartfelt tributes that were paid to Kobe after his death as well as a selection of stunning facts.

Whether you want to be entertained, or to better yourself at work or play, there is so much to enjoy from these reflections throughout his life.

Chapter 1

High School Hero

The son of a famous basketball player, Kobe spent several formative childhood years in Italy.

By the time he returned to high school in the United States, he had learned a lot about basketball, courage, competitiveness, and life. As you will discover, from the very beginning, both his philosophies and determination were strong.

❝

From the beginning, I wanted to be the best.

❞

The Mamba Mentality: How I Play,
MCD 2020

"

My parents are my backbone. Still are. They're the only group that will support you if you score zero or you score 40.

"

As seen on *Newsweek.com*, January 26, 2020, by Scott McDonald

High School Hero

66

When I was three, when my father was playing on the TV, I used to put on my jersey and I'd put some shorts on. And when he would play, I would play, too. I had a little hoop in the living room. When he took time out, I would take time out. Sit down, take some water, wipe the sweat off. Then when he started playing, I'd play again. I would do this for the entire game.

99

On how he copied his father, from an interview on *60 Minutes*, 2001, by Charlie Rose.

66

Italy has always been in my heart.

99

Remembering his childhood years in Italy, during at a sponsor's event in Milan, as seen on *ESPN.com*, September 28, 2001

"

Italy is my home. It's where my dream of playing in the NBA started. This is where I learned the fundamentals.

"

Speaking to *Gazzetta dello Sport*, 2011

The Facts #1

Kobe's parents named him after a type of steak. The beef is from a species of cattle raised in the Kobe region of Japan.

High School Hero

"

Passing, screening, moving off the ball, shooting—all the basics. And if we did scrimmage, we'd scrimmage full court, no dribbles allowed. So that set the foundation for me for how I came to understand the game, and how I now teach the game.

"

Remembering the mini-basket team he played with in Italy, *September Slam*, 2019.

"

There weren't too many black kids running around in Italy at the time.

"

Describing the demography of his neighborhood, during a short documentary by Spike Lee, called *Italian Imports*.

High School Hero

"

The last time I was intimidated was when I was six years old in karate class. I was an orange belt and the instructor ordered me to fight a black belt who was a couple years older and a lot bigger. I was scared s***less. I mean, I was terrified and he kicked my ass. But then I realized he didn't kick my ass as bad as I thought he was going to and that there was nothing really to be afraid of . . .

That was around the time I realized that intimidation didn't really exist if you're in the right frame of mind.

99

As seen on *Newsweek.com*, January 26, 2020, by Scott McDonald

> **"**
>
> As a kid, I would work tirelessly on adding elements to my game. I would see something I liked in person or on film, go practice it immediately, practice it more the next day, and then go out and use it.
>
> **"**

That relentless, obsessive nature showed itself early. *The Mamba Mentality: How I Play*, MCD 2020.

> "
Why am I so attached to Reggio? Because I have so many special memories. Would you have ever thought that one of the NBA's best players could have grown up here? There's nothing farther from Los Angeles. It means that every dream is achievable. "

Explaining the place his Italian neighborhood has in his heart, during a 2016 interview with the Italian newspaper *il Resto del Carlino*.

"

Those were muses to me growing up as a kid.

"

Magic Johnson, Wilt Chamberlain, and other players influenced him hugely as a child, as seen on *NBA.com*, December 15, 2017, by Mike Trudell.

The Facts #2

Kobe's father, Joe "Jellybean" Bryant, was also a professional basketball player. He played in the NBA for eight years with the 76ers, the Clippers, and the Rockets. Then he moved to Europe and played seven seasons in the Italian leagues, taking Kobe and the rest of the family with him.

66

My father taught me at an early age, you've got to think the game. You're not going to be able to do the same thing all the time.

99

On how his father prepared him for the chance of a career-ending injury, as seen in *Off the Dribble* blog, November 23, 2009.

"

I'm telling you, it was something in the pasta.

"

On why he and female basketball star Tamika Catchings did so well after their respective childhoods in Italy, as seen on *WashingtonPost.com*, January 26, 2020, by Meagan Flynn.

High School Hero

"

It was hard because kids weren't speaking English—everybody was speaking slang. So I didn't understand one word! Someone would say 'Stop sweatin me' and I wouldn't know what they were talking about! But basketball's a universal language, so I was able to communicate that way.

"

Recalling his linguistic problems when he returned to the United States on *60 Minutes*, 2001.

"

By reading, by paying attention in class and in practice, by working, I strengthened my focus. By doing all of that, I strengthened my ability to be present and not having a wandering mind.

"

On and off the court, he honed his mind from an early age. *The Mamba Mentality: How I Play*, MCD 2020

66

I've always enjoyed it. In high
school, I had a great Speaking Arts
teacher. She really challenged us to
formulate stories, and share stories,
so I enjoyed that.

99

On the roots of his love of storytelling,
as seen on *USAToday.com*, February 2015,
by Sam Amick.

"

That's my most lasting memory from my high school career— winning the state championship. The high school hadn't won it in over 50 years. So it was big, really big, especially going from 4–20 my freshman year to winning the state title.

"

After leading Lower Merion High School to the 1996 state championship, as seen on *USAToday.com*, May 7, 2002.

❝

When I was growing up it was completely OK to be competitive and to want to be better than the other guy. It was completely understood that I was trying to be better than Tim Thomas coming out of high school, and he was trying to be better than me . . .

That was OK, and now it seems like it's almost passive aggressive—no, I'm not really trying to be better than you, but you really are. As opposed to laying down the gauntlet, and saying, 'No, we're going after each other, even though we're still friends.'

"

On why he thinks there are fewer players with his DNA, as seen on *USAToday.com*, February 2015, by Sam Amick.

❝

I did biblical workouts. I started lifting weights at 17. I mean heavy, hard, can't-feel-your-arms type of lift.

❞

The Mamba Mentality: How I Play,
MCD 2020.

The Facts #3

At Lower Merion high school, Kobe led the basketball team to a state championship, averaging 31 points per game.

66

I believe we still would've won championships in Chicago. That's what I think, but I do feel like everything happens for a reason.

99

On how he nearly joined the Chicago Bulls in 2007, as seen on *hoopshype.com*, June 12, 2018, by Alex Kennedy.

"

From a young age—a very young age—I devoured film and watched everything I could get my hands on. It was always fun to me. Some people, after all, enjoy looking at a watch; others are happier figuring out how the watch works.

"

The Mamba Mentality: How I Play,
MCD 2020.

High School Hero

"

I would have kept playing, that's for sure. I loved basketball so much, but I also wanted to play for AC Milan. If myself, Tracy McGrady, and LeBron James had a soccer ball at our feet instead of a basketball at two years old, with our size, it could have been something.

"

Admitting he could have become a soccer star, while chatting with the *Chicago Tribune* in 2016.

"

On this day 18 years ago the Hornets told me right after they drafted me that they had no use for me and were going to trade me.

"

Remembering his rejection, as seen on *Twitter*, July 1, 2014.

66

Charlotte never wanted me. [Hornets coach Dave] Cowens told me he didn't want me. It wasn't a question of me even playing here. They had a couple of guards already, a couple small forwards already. So it wasn't like I would be off the bench much.

99

CBSSports.com, April 4, 2016, by Zach Harper

❝

I didn't score a point the whole summer. Not one point. Not a free throw, not a layup. Nothing, zero points the whole summer. My father came up to me afterwards and said, son, don't worry about it. We're going to love you if you score zero or 50.

❞

Recalling a pivotal summer in Philadelphia, during a 2001 interview with Charlie Rose on *60 Minutes*.

39

"

I'd be a Hornet.

"

His straightforward response when asked,
in 1996, what would have happened if the
trade deal had fallen through, as seen on
Charlotte Observer, January 26, 2020,
by Rick Bonnell.

The Facts #4

He took the R&B star Brandy Norwood to his high school prom.

Chapter 2

The Rookie Rises

Drafted to the NBA at the tender age of 17, Kobe quickly established a reputation as a fearless, intimidating, and envied player.

He was in no mood to merely make up the numbers. Although he was outspoken, he was his own biggest critic and, in search of sporting perfection, showed a determination to find and correct his own mistakes and weaknesses.

The Rookie Rises

"

It wasn't that people thought I was soft. It was more of a street credibility thing: 'He grew up in Italy. He's not one of us.'

"

Remembering the response of Americans when he returned to the United States, as seen on *GQ.com*, February 18, 2015, by Chuck Klosterman

“

I mean, I had grown up watching basketball. I quickly transitioned from smiley kid to killer instinct.

”

He toughened up fast. *CBSSports.com*, April 4, 2016, by Zach Harper

66

Just getting drafted. Having a chance to hear a commissioner call my name, put on a hat, and finally be in the NBA.

99

Speaking to NBC in 1997, he reveals the highlight of his career so far.

"

I was willing to do way more than anyone else. That was the fun part for me.

"

The Mamba Mentality: How I Play,
MCD 2020.

> **"**
> I was like a wild horse that had the potential to become Secretariat, but who was just too f***ing wild. So part of that was [Phil Jackson] trying to tame me.
> **"**

Admitting he was a challenge to coach, as seen on *wealthygorilla.com*, by Dan Western

66

It wasn't that intimidating—
basketball is basketball. You just
go out there and have fun. **99**

Explaining to Cindy Crawford why he wasn't
nervous for his debut at 18, NBC, 1997.

66

When it came to basketball, I had no fear. I wasn't scared of missing, looking bad, or being embarrassed.

99

As seen on *CNN*, January 27, 2020

"

Kids go to school to be doctors or lawyers, so forth and so on, and that's where they study. My place to study is from the best.

"

On why he was happy to move straight from school to the NBA, as seen on *GiveMeSport.com*, January 27, 2020, by Kobe Tong.

The Rookie Rises

66

I'm going out there to answer a challenge that I put to myself since the ninth grade. I had said to myself that if I had the option to skip college and go straight to the NBA, I would. The option came my way, and I took advantage.

99

On being drafted to Charlotte Hornets, as seen on *ESPN.com*, June 1, 2010, by Justin Verrier.

"

When I first came into the league, I really didn't know what to expect. I knew I had a lot to learn. I felt I was ready but I needed to improve a lot. In the process, I went through a lot of ups and downs. Failed miserably a couple of times but that comes with the territory. I had to pick myself up and go back out and try again.

"

Interviewed by KCAL in 2002

The Rookie Rises

66

I say 'Thank you for the feedback.' Everybody has an opinion, everybody sees you at a different level. So I'm going to listen, see what I need to work on, and go out there and work on my skills. Next time they see me play, I'm going to say, 'Hey look, I worked on it.' Now what?

99

His response to the critics who said he wasn't ready for the league, as seen on *ESPN*, 1996.

"

To me it was a really, really big moment; it was a really, really big deal. And it kind of proved to me that hard work and the work you do in the off-season is going to pay dividends for you in-season.

"

Putting into context the famous 1997 game when he threw four "airballs" against Utah Jazz, as seen on *CBSsports.com*, Jan 16, 2016, by Zach Harper

"

It's only human nature that it's going to be there every once in a while.

"

Speaking about the jealousy of his teammates during an interview with Peter Vecsey, 1999.

The Facts #5

When he was drafted out of high school, his parents had to sign his contract, because he was not yet 18. He was the first guard to be drafted straight out of high school.

66

Once you know what failure feels like, determination chases success.

99

Newsweek, January 2020

"

During my rookie year, at first, some scouting reports said I wasn't tough. The first time I went to the basket in games, I'd get hit and the defense would think they had me. I'd come back the very next play and pick up an offensive foul just to send them a message.

"

Remembering his early reputation, as seen on *FoxNews.com*, January 29, 2020.

The Rookie Rises

"

When you first come into the league, you're trying to prove yourself as an individual, do things to assert yourself and establish yourself.

"

Off the Dribble, November 23, 2009

66

So, the game is so beautiful. It's so pure—the smell of a ball, the smell of the sneakers, the squeaking of the court, the sound that the nets make when you shoot a basket and it goes through the hole.

99

On why he fell in love with basketball, *CBSsports.com*, October 25, 2014, by Ken Berger.

The Rookie Rises

66

Well, look, I'll take that 2000–01 Lakers squad we had against any team in the history of this game. Against any team.

99

hoopshype.com, June 12, 2018, by Alex Kennedy

66

I've shot too much from the time I was eight years old, but 'too much' is a matter of perspective. Some people thought Mozart had too many notes in his compositions. Let me put it this way: I *entertain* people who say I shoot too much. I find it very interesting. Going back to Mozart, he responded to critics by saying there were neither too many notes or too few. There were as many as necessary.

99

GQ.com February 18, 2015, by Chuck Klosterman

The Rookie Rises

"

Oh, I could tell. I could tell. From playing for so many years, you can sort of sense that kind of stuff. You can feel that nervous energy all over them.

"

On whether he noticed that rookies were nervous when they faced him on the court. *hoopshype.com*, June 12, 2018, by Alex Kennedy

66

I can swing too far on the nice side or on the bad-cop side. Being a leader, it's the art of trying to find the balance, the right times with each individual player and what they need at that moment. It requires looking outward as opposed to looking inside.

99

On captaincy, *USAToday.com*, February 2015, by Sam Amick

66

I think I'm really fortunate because
I really love what I do. They're
players who do it because they're
good at it or use it as a means
just to provide or accolades or
adoration. That's a different kind
of motivation. When you do
something that you truly, truly love
doing, you find yourself wanting to
do it all the time.

99

Off the Dribble, November 23, 2009

"

We psyche ourselves up too much. Like if you try to talk yourself into, 'Oh, this is a big moment, this is a big shot,' you're putting a lot of pressure on yourself. You shot that shot hundreds and thousands of times. Just shoot another one.

"

His tip on how to keep the mind quiet, *Jimmy Kimmel Live*, 2018

The Rookie Rises

“

Whether it's sponsorships or
the limelight or distractions with
social media, there are a lot of
different things that can pull you
in different directions.

”

hoopshype.com, June 12, 2018,
by Alex Kennedy

"

Not even in my dreams. That was something that just happened. It's tough to explain. It's just one of those things.

"

When he scored 81 points in a game against the Toronto Raptors in 2006, as seen on *Newsweek*.

The Rookie Rises

"

That Toronto game, there was a calmness to it. Like a stillness. Nothing mattered to me other than what was right in front of me. It wasn't anybody in the crowd, or what an opponent may say or do. It was just about the play right in front of me, and I was able to . . . maintain that throughout.

"

Theundefeated.com, February 16, 2018, by Aaron Dodson

The Facts #6

In 1996, he was the youngest player in NBA history at that point: 18 years, two months, and 11 days.

In 1997, he became the youngest player to ever win the NBA Slam Dunk Contest.

66

Better learn not to talk to me.
You shake the tree, a leopard's
gonna fall out.

99

Warning the world not to summon his
aggression, as seen on *wealthygorilla.com*,
by Dan Western.

66

I just want people to say: 'That guy can play. We saw him grow from 17 years old, to 20, to 25, and he's blossomed into a pretty good basketball player.

99

On how he wanted to be regarded 20 years into the future, during a 1999 interview with Doc Rivers on *TNT Sports*.

Chapter 3

All-Star Years

Winning five NBA titles and two Olympic gold medals, and a Most Valuable Player (MVP) award, Kobe's glory years with the LA Lakers were truly golden.

His approach to the game was truly ruthless, and he was unforgiving toward anyone he felt was not pulling his weight. He was happy to tread on toes on the path to legendary status.

"

There is only one team like
the Lakers.

"

GQ.com, February 18, 2015,
by Chuck Klosterman

"
I am a maniacal worker, and if you're not working as hard as I am, I am going to let you know about it.

"

On how outspoken he was to teammates, *GQ.com*, February 18, 2015, by Chuck Klosterman

66

I don't want to be the next Michael Jordan, I only want to be Kobe Bryant.

99

Enough said, *Newsweek*, January 26 ,2020, by Scott McDonald.

"

My mentality is I never waste my time arguing things that I definitively cannot win. So I don't waste my time even debating that kind of stuff. Because for every argument somebody makes for me being the best, there's always somebody who makes an argument for LeBron being the best, or Jordan, or whoever . . . If I can't win definitively, I'm not gonna waste my energy on it.

"

On his opinion of who's the greatest, him or LeBron James, *theundefeated.com*, February 16, 2018

66

One thing you gotta know about me is I have absolutely no filter. I have no problem saying what the hell I think of someone.

99

As seen on *popculture.com*,
February 28, 2020, by Brian Jones

"

The antisocial has become social
#mambatweets.

*Announcing his arrival in style, with his
first tweet on* Twitter, *January 4, 2013*

"

❝

Random tears of devastation and doubt mixed with inner determination and will #countonfamily #countonprayer THANKU #vicodintweets comin ha!

❞

After he ruptured his Achilles tendon, on *Twitter*, April 2013

"

The first time I was getting ready
to face Jordan, I had a teammate,
he goes, 'Hey, you want some
advice? Whatever you do, don't
look him in the eye.' Wait, excuse
me? Why the hell would I not look
him in the eye? I don't think my
teammate understood that I'm
THAT, too. Can't . . . look me in
the eye either, buddy.

"

From the Showtime/CBS Sports documentary
Kobe Bryant's Muse, 2015

"

Amnesty THAT.

"

After Dallas Mavericks owner Mark Cuban suggested the Lakers could amnesty him, Bryant and the Lakers torched the Mavericks in the next game. *Twitter*, February 24 2013.

66

Over the years, my routine might have changed some but my philosophy never did. If something has worked for other greats before you, and if something is working for you, why change it up and embrace some new fad? Stick with what works, even if it's unpopular.

99

The Mamba Mentality: How I Play, MCD, 2020

66

The thing that I'm afraid of is not winning another championship.

99

During an appearance on CMI
(*Chris Myers Interview*), 2006.

The Facts #7

He made the NBA All-Star Game a total of 18 times. The only player with more selections is Kareem Abdul-Jabbar, who played in 19.

66

We had a player in training camp actually named Gelabale. He was a young player, but he had been in the league before. I could tell he was really nervous. We'd had a little altercation when he was playing for Seattle and now he was in training camp with me on the Lakers and he's face-to-face with me every day, knowing that I hadn't forgotten what happened and that I was never going to forget. I could tell that he was really, really nervous and I made it a point to make his training camp absolute hell. **99**

It was always a good plan to not get on the wrong side of Kobe, as he demonstrated here, *hoopshype. com*, June 12, 2018, by Alex Kennedy.

"

In 2008, 2009, 2010 [with the Lakers] it became more about the guys in the locker room, it became more observing where they are emotionally, whereas before you're just thinking about where I'm at, how can I get results. It's a very big difference—it's a small shift, but it makes a big difference. Because once you open your eyes and start looking around you, you start picking up things that are very obvious.

"

On captaincy, *USAToday.com*, February 2015, by Sam Amick.

❝

#Vino.

❞

Announcing a new nickname for himself,
reflecting that he felt he was getting better
with age. *Twitter*, March 4, 2013

❝

Does my nature make me less enjoyable to play with? Of course. Of course it does. Is it possible that some top players in the league are intimidated by that? Yes.

❞

GQ.com, February 18, 2015, by Chuck Klosterman

66

Count to 5.

99

His reply to a fan who asked, "What do you say to
people who call you a selfish basketball player?"
Twitter, June 6, 2015

"

The fact that we can have a collection of athletes that come from different backgrounds, with different beliefs, different political views, but yet can figure out a way to understand each other, how to work well with each other toward a common goal . . . there's no better metaphor for life than that.

"

Sport imitating life, *NBA.com*,
December 15, 2017, by Mike Trudell

"

I enjoy building. I enjoy the process of putting the puzzle together, and then the by-product of that, the consequence of that, is beating somebody. That becomes the cherry on top, the icing on the cake. But the thing that's most enjoyable to me is not actually beating you. It's the process of coming up with the blueprint of beating you that I enjoy.

"

Outlining the difference between his and Michael Jordan's competitive spirits, *USAToday.com*, February 2015, by Sam Amick

66

I knew what I could have done individually. I could have gone to another team and averaged 35 points a game. I could have gone anywhere and destroyed people. I gave that up to win championships.

99

On allegations he was selfish, *GQ.com*, February 18, 2015, by Chuck Klosterman

The Facts #8

He was the first NBA player to ever play 20 seasons with the same team.

Kobe is the only NBA player in history to have two separate numbers retired by one team, as he wore both No. 8 and No. 24 with the Los Angeles Lakers.

66

That's not what I do, man. I've got to take the good times with the bad, man. You can't ask to be the leader of the franchise, and then when the franchise hits rough times, you say, 'All right, thank you. Peace.'

99

On rumors he wanted to leave the Lakers, *USAToday.com*, February 2015, by Sam Amick

66

Everything negative—pressure,
challenges—is all an opportunity
for me to rise.

99

As seen on *bbc.co.uk*, January 26, 2020

All-Star Years

"

It was kind of a snap shot of the arc of my career, really. The struggles to start. The ebbs and flows throughout the course of the game. Physically being tired but pushing through. That perseverance. The footwork that was there, the fundamentals of the game were there. But also the emotional strengths to be able to have the inner confidence that this thing will turn around.

"

His 60-point game against Utah Jazz was a special one, as he told *NBA.com*, December 15, 2017, by Mike Trudell.

66

Oh, yeah. But the things that make a person average are also problems. The things that make someone not good at anything at all are a problem. If you want to be the greatest of all time at something, there's going to be a negative side to that.

99

Admitting that there is a downside to his approach, *GQ.com*, February 18, 2015, by Chuck Klosterman

Chapter 4

Get in the Zone

As well as being one of basketball's most decorated and famous players, Kobe was also known for his words and thoughts.

His 'Mamba Mentality' was uncompromising, unabashed, and inspiring to millions. It also pushed the man himself to increasingly great heights. Put simply, failure was not an option.

66

If you do not believe in yourself,
no one will do it for you.

99

Newsweek, January 26 2020,
by Scott McDonald

"

I called John Williams in 2008 . . .
there are so many instruments and
all these different sections, from the
woodwinds to the percussion to the
horns and all sorts of stuff. And he has
to lead all of those sections, all of those
people, to create one harmonious
sound . . . I sat down with him for a bit
and picked his brain about it, because
I felt like there were a lot of similarities
between what he does and what I have
to do on the basketball court.

"

hoopshype.com, June 12, 2018, by Alex Kennedy

"

The moment you give up
is the moment you let
someone else win.

"

As seen on *clutchpoints.com*,
June 14, 2020, by Kriel Ibarrola

" I've never played for the money. It's never moved me. Money can come and go. I have a perspective about finances. The family is fine. What is more money going to bring other than more money? "

On why he played so long,
chinadaily.com, May 8

Get in the Zone

66

I have friends. But being a 'great friend' is something I will never be. I can be a good friend. But not a great friend. A great friend will call you every day and remember your birthday. I'll get so wrapped up in my s**t, I'll never remember that stuff. And the people who are my friends understand this, and they're usually the same way.

99

GQ.com, February 18, 2015, by Chuck Klosterman

The Facts #9

Kobe was the 2008 NBA Most Valuable Player (MVP) and two-time NBA Finals MVP. He was also NBA scoring champion twice and a two-time Olympic champion.

Get in the Zone

66

When ur game take a s*i* .
Flush it. Get up and move on
#mambaism.

99

Literally, dispensing advice on *Twitter*,
March 23, 2013

"

When my sisters heard that, they just laughed! They just laughed at me, like: 'Kobe? Peanut head? Get out of here!' I'm pretty much thinking the same thing. I don't see how people see my in that light but thank you, I appreciate it!

"

On his reputation as the most "sexy, eligible bachelor in basketball," *Access Hollywood*, 1999

"

It is a continuous search to attempt to be better now than you were.

"

On the quest for perfection, *Washington Post*, January 26, 2020, by Jerry Brewer

" Be sad. Be mad. Be frustrated. Scream. Cry. Sulk. When you wake up you will think it was just a nightmare only to realize it's all too real. You will be angry and wish for the day back, the game back, THAT play back. But reality gives nothing back and nor should you. **"**

His advice to Gordon Hayward following his injury, *Instagram*, 2017

"

If you're afraid to fail, then you're probably going to fail.

"

A philosophy for success, as seen on *CNN*, January 26, 2020

66

A lot of people say they want to be great, but they're not willing to make the sacrifices necessary to achieve greatness. They have other concerns, whether important or not, and they spread themselves out. That's totally fine. After all, greatness is not for everybody.

99

The Mamba Mentality: How I Play,
MCD, 2020

"

If I had a game where I had 60 points, I wouldn't look at the things I did right; I'd try to find every little thing that I did wrong and look at the issues I might have in the next game.

"

hoopshype.com, June 12, 2018, by Alex Kennedy

The Facts #10

He retired as the all-time highest scoring Laker, and the fourth-highest scoring player in NBA history, with 33,643 career points.

Get in the Zone

"I'm not going to say our marriage is perfect, by any stretch of the imagination," Kobe says. "We still fight, just like every married couple. But you know, my reputation as an athlete is that I'm extremely determined, and that I will work my ass off. How could I do that in my professional life if I wasn't like that in my personal life, when it affects my kids? It wouldn't make any sense.

GQ.com, February 18, 2015,
by Chuck Klosterman

"

Have a good time. Life is too short to get bogged down and be discouraged. You have to keep moving. You have to keep going. Put one foot in front of the other, smile, and just keep on rolling.

"

GiveMeSport.com, January 27 2020, by Kobe Tong

Get in the Zone

66

There's a choice that we have to make as people, as individuals. If you want to be great at something, there's a choice you have to make. We all can be masters at our craft, but you have to make a choice. What I mean by that is, there are inherent sacrifices that come along with that. Family time, hanging out with friends, being a great friend, being a great son, nephew, whatever the case may be. There are sacrifices that come along with making that decision.

99

Revealing his ruthlessness as friend and relative, as seen on *NYTimes.com*, January 27, 2020

"

I had to figure out how to teach.
Parenting is teaching. How do
you teach your children to be
upstanding citizens? How do
you teach them that they can
accomplish what they set out to
accomplish? How do you teach is
the most important thing.

"

On becoming a dad, *NBA.com*,
December 15, 2017, by Mike Trudell

"

The truth is, if you want to be beloved in Los Angeles, you have to win championships. That's it. I mean, you can be the greatest guy in the world, but if you don't hang banners here in LA, then you'll just be a good guy who is forgotten the next year or whenever you retire.

"

There's only one way to succeed in LA—and that is to succeed, *hoopshype.com*, June 12, 2018, by Alex Kennedy

Get in the Zone

"

We all have moments where we all
have that kind of villain inside. We
all have those hero moments, as
well. But I think the important thing
to understand is you take those
dark emotions and you use them
to create something great. And
not to run from those things.

"

Coming to terms with his darker side,
CBSsports.com, January 16, 2016, by Zach Harper

The Facts #11

When he retired at the end of the
2015 season, he had been in the NBA
for more than half his life.

Get in the Zone

"

God don't give us nothing we can't handle. So just know you're in our thoughts, you're in our prayers, and you'll be just fine. Mamba mentality this thing all the way through.

"

His message in a video with one of his fans, Timbo Thymes, whose mother had been diagnosed with breast cancer.
Twitter, January 5, 2020

66

I love my wife with all my heart.
She's my backbone.

99

Paying tribute to Vanessa, *Mirror.co.uk*,
January 27, 2020, by Emmeline Saunders

Get in the Zone

66

If I needed to get keyed up, I listened to hard music. If I needed to soothe myself, I might play the same soundtrack I listened to on the bus in high school to put me back in that place.

99

The Mamba Mentality: How I Play, MCD, 2020

66

I'm crazy. Ha, ha, ha. I love playing.
I enjoy it. It's weird. You go from as
a kid loving the game, thinking you
will be able to play forever to being
where I am now and understanding
there is some finality to it.

99

On why he played so long,
Chinadaily.com, May 5, 2015

Get in the Zone

“

Those times when you get up early and you work hard, those times when you stay up late and you work hard, those times when you don't feel like working, you're too tired, you don't want to push yourself, but you do it anyway. That is actually the dream. That's the dream. It's not the destination, it's the journey. **”**

From his jersey retirement speech, *LATimes.com*, 2017

" As I sit here now, when I take off my shoe and I look down at my scar, I see beauty in it. I see all the hard work, all the sacrifices. I see the journey that it took to get back to this point of being healthy. And I see beauty in that struggle. That's what makes it beautiful. **"**

As seen on *DailyMail.co.uk*, January 31, 2020

"

I'm probably not the flag bearer for being really careful about what you eat. I just try to be mindful, that's all.

"

Admitting he was not the healthiest of eaters, *Access Hollywood*, 2009

The Facts #12

In his final game, Kobe took 50 shots,
the most of any player since 1967.

“

We hated those guys. We felt like they were so arrogant. It was always like, 'We could beat you guys any time we want.' That sort of thing . . .

”

On the rivalry between the Los Angeles Lakers and Phoenix Suns, *theundefeated.com*, 2018

66

Despite fear, finish the job.

99

As seen on *Newsweek*, January 26, 2020,
by Scott McDonald

"

In the end it's just about getting better. Focus on your game. That's it.

"

His philosophy in a nutshell, *NBA.com*, December 15, 2017, by Mike Trudell

"
Mamba out.

"

His final words before his retirement,
as seen on *BruteImpact.com*

Chapter 5

The Charity Champ

After he retired from basketball, Kobe channeled his energy into the charity and business ventures he had already launched.

Whether it was being nominated for an Oscar or meeting homeless people on the street, he approached his new ventures with the same vigor and determination that he had shown during his two decades on the court.

The Charity Champ

66

You can't be a business person if
the decisions that you make are
held hostage by the perception
that others have of you. You can't
be a successful businessman
from my point of view and sit in a
room with these owners—who are
phenomenal business people—and
have a peer-to-peer conversation,
if they know at the end of the
day you're going to capitulate
to public perception.

99

CBSsports.com, Oct 25, 2014, by Ken Berger

"

Yes, it's important to see those returns, right? But it's also important to have great opportunity, great relationships with our investors, great opportunities with our entrepreneurs to help them grow and put them in situations where they can be successful.

"

As seen on *CNN.com*, January 30, 2020, by Clare Duffy and Alexis Benveniste

The Charity Champ

"

You kidding me? No. No. No.

"

On whether, as a player, he would have dreamed of becoming an award-winning media executive and content producer. *theundefeated.com*, October 18, 2018, by Jerry Bembry

66

The most important thing is to try and inspire people so that they can be great in whatever they want to do.

99

As seen on *Clutchpoints.com*, June 14, 2020, by Kriel Ibarrola

The Charity Champ

"

It feels wonderful. Being at the Oscar luncheon, and having a chance to sit with Steven Spielberg, and Octavia Spencer, and Meryl Streep . . . all those beautiful minds that I've admired for so many years is awesome . . . it's a great experience.

"

On how it feels to be an Oscar nominee, *theundefeated.com*, 2018.

"

I can't relate to lazy people. We don't speak the same language. I don't understand you. I don't want to understand you.

"

As seen on *Inc.com*, January 26, 2020

The Charity Champ

"

Hey, what's up, Coach White?
Listen, I understand you're a big
fan, but the truth is that the work
you do makes you the hero.

"

A recorded message for the deaf high
school basketball coach Sekoe White,
on *Rachael Ray Show*, 2019

“

It's a belief that we all have a responsibility to each other, to help one another. It's the fundamental belief. If we have an opportunity to do that, then it's our responsibility as people to help one another. And that's it, it's as simple as that.

”

Explaining why he appeared on *The View* to support six-year-old Bryson Thompson, who has epilepsy, 2018.

The Charity Champ

"

My brain . . . it cannot process
failure. It will not process failure.
Because if I sit there and have to
face myself and tell myself, 'You're
a failure' . . . I think that's almost
worse than death.

"

As seen on *NBA.com*, January 30, 2020

"

Originally, I thought the term, Mamba Mentality was only a tricky hashtag that I would begin on Twitter. Something memorable and witty. However, it took off from there and then came to signify a great deal more. The mindset is not about searching an outcome—it is about the practice of getting this outcome. It's all about the journey as well as the strategy. It is a method of life.

"

Kobe Bryant: The Inspirational Story of One of the Greatest Basketball Players of All Time, March 28, 2019, by Patrick Thompson

The Charity Champ

"

On my way to games, I noticed children and families living on the streets, blocks away from where I play.

"

Describing his awakening to the issue of homelessness, *HuffPost.com*, June 7, 2011

"

You have to do something that carries a little bit more weight to it, a little more significance, a little more purpose to it.

"

On his charity work, *HuffPost.com*, June 7, 2011

"

We want to help homeless
youth kick butt.

"

On his charity work, *LATimes.com*,
September 12, 2012, by Ben Bolch

Go. See. This. Museum. There is no greater testament to this country than the stories in this building. Honored to be a part of it.

Through the Kobe and Vanessa Bryant Family Foundation, Bryant became a milestone donor, contributing $1 million or more, to the Smithsonian's National Museum of African American History and Culture, *Instagram*, September 24, 2016.

The Charity Champ

"

I was trying to hear some of their stories and some of their backgrounds and how they got to this position. I wanted to know when that switch went off inside of them and they said, 'I need help; I want to turn my life around.' It gave me great perspective.

"

On why he chose to meet homeless people, *ESPN.com*, September 12, 2012, by Arash Markazi

The Facts #13

In January 2000, he released a single called "K.O.B.E.," which featured him rapping about his love for "basketball, beats, and broads."

In 2018, he won an Oscar for best short animated film for Dear Basketball, a five-minute movie based on a love letter to the sport he had written in 2015.

The Charity Champ

"

It's funny, because the reaction is always the same, where everybody is a little taken aback, because nobody has really had a chance to think about their own process and how they do things. It winds up being a therapeutic experience. You get a chance to think, 'How did I do this?'

"

On his habit of cold-calling powerful people to learn from them, *USAToday.com*, February 2015, by Sam Amick

"

It's hard, because you're always working, you're always fine-tuning things, you never believe anything is as it should be and you always want to continue to rework things. Sometimes, I refer to it as, like, a disease or a curse or an affliction. It can feel like that!

"

On how his obsessive nature dovetails in business, *hoopshype.com*, June 12, 2018, by Alex Kennedy

The Charity Champ

"

If we're going to do anything, whether it's the Muse film or The Mamba Mentality book, it has to have a reason for existing. So the layers I put on it, if it's me at 12 years old and I'm reading a book, what would I want to read?

"

theundefeated.com, October 18, 2018, by Jerry Bembry

66

The industry I'm in now, with creativity . . . you don't want to strangle the creative process. You want to be able to give freedom and the ability to grow. So my job really is just making sure we find the right talent, people that are obsessive and love what they do, and creating an environment in which I put them in the best possible situation to grow. And that is it.

99

Outlining the difference in relationship with teammates in sport and business, *NBA.com*, December 15, 2017, by Mike Trudell

"

I don't want to be too cheesy
and quote Spider-Man, but
with great power comes
great responsibility.

"

His superhero code for charity and business,
LakersNation.com, 2013

66

You know, I've been fortunate
to play in Los Angeles, where
there are a lot of people like me.
Actors. Musicians. Businessmen.
Obsessives. People who feel like
God put them on earth to do
whatever it is that they do.

99

GQ.com, February 18, 2015,
by Chuck Klosterman

The Charity Champ

"

Well, the goal for us here at the studio is always the same: It's about quality above quantity . . . quality above all else. That's our focus every day.

"

Setting the bar high for his projects, *hoopshype.com*, June 12, 2018, by Alex Kennedy

"

I believe the messages I'm trying to convey are universal. It doesn't matter how old you are or where you come from or what language you speak. Mamba Mentality is for everyone.

"

kickz.com, October 23, 2017

The Charity Champ

"

[The homelessness] issue is one that kind of gets pushed on the back burner, because it's easy to point the blame at those who are homeless and say, 'Well, you made that bad decision. This is where you are. It's your fault.' In life, we all make mistakes and to stand back and allow someone to live that way and kind of wash your hands of it . . . that's not right.

"

LakersNation.com, 2013

"

We have a very, very solid team
here. What we do is build and
find partners that believe in the
core philosophy that sports is
the greatest metaphor for life.
If they believe that and can see
the potential in that, they will
be great partners.

"

NBA.com, December 15, 2017,
by Mike Trudell

The Charity Champ

"

At some point, it has to become about something more than just winning championships, right?
It has to become about something more—about how you've helped the next generation and how you've given back to the game.

"

On his legacy, *hoopshype.com*,
June 12, 2018, by Alex Kennedy

"

Losing is losing, there aren't different degrees of losing. You either win a championship or you're s**t. It's very black and white to me.

"

As seen on *wealthygorilla.com*, by Dan Western

The Charity Champ

"

Like *Dear Basketball*, which is
a basketball film. But yet I have
people come up to me and say
'I wasn't a basketball fan at all, I
wasn't thinking about basketball,
but that film moved me.' If we
can do that, I feel like we're
doing our jobs.

"

As seen on *NYPost.com*, January 29, 2020

" Just put one foot in front of the other, go on to the next thing, and try to do something better the next day than you did the last day. **"**

USAToday.com, February 2015, by Sam Amick

The Charity Champ

"

Continuing to move the game forward @KingJames. Much respect my brother.

"

Writing on *Twitter*, just 15 hours before he died, Kobe pays tribute to Lakers' LeBron James after he passed his points record. *Twitter*, January 26, 2020

"

I'm so excited to see what God has in store for us as a family now that one chapter is closing and new ones are opening. **"**

After he retired *Mirror.co.uk*,
January 27 2020, by Emmeline Saunders

Chapter 6

Feel the Love

When Kobe died in a helicopter crash in January 2020, along with his daughter Gianna, the worlds of sport and show business mourned the passing of a legend.

The quantity and sincerity of the tributes that flooded in reflected the extraordinary contribution he had made during the 41 years of his life.

Feel the Love

66

We're all feeling crazy sadness right now. Because earlier today Los Angeles, America, and the whole wide world lost a hero. We're literally standing here heartbroken in the house that Kobe Bryant built.

99

Alicia Keys, speaking at the Grammy Awards, which were held at the Staples Center, the Los Angeles Lakers' stadium, *BBC.co.uk*

66

Kobe, We love you brother.
We're praying for your family
and appreciate the life you've
lived and all the inspiration
you gave.

99

Kanye West, *Instagram*, January 26, 2020

Feel the Love

66

You had the magical ability of bringing people together, through sports and through your soul.
We feel you so heavily today,
I know you can feel us, too.

99

Kendall Jenner, *Instagram*, January 26, 2020

66
You always encouraged me
Mamba. Gave me some of the
best quotes that we smile about
to this day.
99

Justin Bieber, *Instagram*, January 26, 2020

Feel the Love

> " I have no words . . . All my love for Kobe's family and friends. It was a pleasure to meet you and share good times together. You were a genius like few others. "

Soccer ace Lionel Messi,
Instagram, January 27, 2020

" Kobe was a true legend and inspiration to so many. Sending my condolences to his family and friends and the families of all who lost their lives in the crash. RIP Legend. **"**

Real Madrid's superstar Cristiano Ronaldo, January 26, 2020

Feel the Love

> **Mamba, you were taken away from us too soon. Your next chapter of life was just beginning. But now it is time for us to continue your legacy. You said yourself that everything negative—pressure, challenges— is all an opportunity for me to rise. So we now take that sage advice to now rise from anguish and begin with the healing.**

Shaquille O'Neal, *The New York Times*, 2020

The Facts #14

The NBA postponed the Lakers' game against the Clippers two days Kobe's death—the first time an NBA game had been postponed for any reason since the 2013 Boston Marathon bombing led to the postponement of a Celtics game.

Feel the Love

> **"** Everyone wanted to talk about the comparisons between him and I. I just wanted to talk about Kobe. **"**

Michael Jordan, speaking at
the memorial, 2020

66

God knew they couldn't be on this earth without each other. He had to bring them home together. 99

Vanessa Bryant, on Kobe and their daughter Gianna, *Twitter*, 2020

> **"**
> Kobe was a legend on the court and just getting started in what would have been just as meaningful a second act. **"**

Barack Obama, *Twitter*, 2020

66

Kobe Bryant grew up here and for us all he was from Reggio Emilia. He left us today. A basketball legend whom our whole city will remember forever with affection and gratitude.

99

Luca Vecchi, the mayor of Reggio Emilia— one of the Italian cities where the Bryants had lived, writing on Facebook, as seen in *WashingtonPost.com*, January 26, 2020

"

Kobe is G. Will always be remembered. A sad day.

Idris Elba, *Twitter*, 2020

"

The Facts #15

Basketball legends Michael Jordan, Magic Johnson, Shaquille O'Neal, Jerry West, and Kareem Abdul-Jabbar attended the memorial service at the Staples Center alongside contemporary stars, including Stephen Curry, James Harden, and Russell Westbrook.

66

Kobe was not only an icon in the sports arena, he was a man of the world and touched so many lives and communities in the most positive ways.

99

NBA Hall of Famer, Larry Bird, *Sky News*, January 26, 2020

66

Kobe didn't care about night life or anything. He only had one interest. His only focus was to be the best that he could be. And in his mind that meant challenging Michael Jordan. People can argue how close he actually came, but there's no question that he fulfilled pretty much all of his dreams.

99

Del Harris, who coached Kobe for his first two NBA seasons and the start of his third. *The New York Times*, 2017

Feel the Love

&&

We knew him as the kid phenom
straight from high school. He hit
the league and murked it, [then] he
became a champion. It's very hard
to become a champion. He did it
again and then again.

,,

Lil Wayne, *MTV*, March 2020

" It's very difficult for me to put in words how I feel. Kobe was an incredible family man, he loved his wife and daughters, he was an incredible athlete, he inspired a whole generation. This loss is hard to comprehend. **"**

Kareem Abdul-Jabbar, who played for the Lakers from 1975–89, *BBC*, January 27, 2020

Feel the Love

> **"** Kobe was a leader of our game, a mentor to both male and female players. Words can't express the impact that he had on the game of basketball. **"**

Former LA Lakers president Magic Johnson, a five-time NBA champion in the 1980s, *Twitter*, January 27, 2020